The
Lausanne
Covenant

An Exposition and Commentary
by John Stott

World Wide Publications
1313 Hennepin Avenue
Minneapolis, Minnesota 55403

A theologian who teaches in Asia has written about the Lausanne Covenant, "History may show this Covenant to be the most significant ecumenical confession on evangelism that the church has ever produced." It is a bold statement. As he says, only history will tell. In the meantime, while we wait history's verdict, how did it come to be written?

A first and fairly short statement was produced two or three months before the Congress and submitted by mail to a number of advisers. Already this document may truly be said to have come out of the Congress (although the Congress had not yet assembled), because it reflected the contributions of the main speakers whose papers had been published in advance. The document was revised in the light of the advisers' comments, and this revision was further revised at Lausanne by the drafting committee. So what was submitted to all participants in the middle of the Congress was the third draft. They were invited to send in their contributions, either as individuals or as groups, and they responded with great diligence. Many hundreds of submissions were received (in the official languages), translated into English, sorted and studied. Some proposed amendments canceled each other out, but the drafting committee incorporated all they could, while at the same time insuring that the final document was a recognizable revision of the draft submitted to participants. It may truly be said, then, that the Lausanne Covenant expresses a consensus of the mind and mood of the Lausanne Congress.

The word "covenant" is not used in its technical, biblical sense, but in the ordinary sense of a binding contract. For example, in seventeenth century Scotland there were the famous "Covenanters" who bound themselves by a "solemn league and covenant" to maintain the freedom of the church. The reason the expression "Lausanne Covenant" was chosen in preference to "Lausanne Declaration" is that we wanted to do more than find an agreed formula of words. We were determined not just to declare something, but to do something, namely to commit ourselves to the task of world evangelization.

The fifteen sections or paragraphs into which the Covenant is divided are all packed fairly tight with content. So the purpose of this exposition and commentary is to help to "unpack" it, to draw out both the meaning and the implications of what it says. Inevitably this is a personal interpretation, and does not carry the authority of the Planning Committee. Nevertheless, a conscientious attempt has been made to set it in the context of the Congress papers, addresses and discussion, and to let the Covenant speak for itself. It is for this reason that the full text appears twice, first at the head of each section, and secondly broken up into sentences and incorporated into the commentary (in italics).

The same desire to let the Covenant speak for itself has led to the decision to omit a bibliography and references to other literature. The only quotations are from Congress papers and addresses (which are printed in full in the official Compendium) and from the Revised Standard Version of the Bible. Biblical references are numerous, for the Covenant will commend itself only in so far as it can show itself to be a true expression of biblical teaching and principles.

Bishop Jack Dain, Chairman of the Planning Committee, has referred to Lausanne as "a process, not just an event." One important aspect of the continuing process will be the study of the Covenant both by individuals and by groups. In order to facilitate discussion, a series of questions has been added at the end of each chapter.

John Stott
(September, 1974)

The Introduction to the text of the Covenant is not just a formal preamble; it describes the context within which the Covenant must be read and interpreted. It says something important about who the participants were, what the mood of the Congress was and how the Covenant came into being.

a. The Lausanne participants

We who were *participants in the International Congress on World Evangelization at Lausanne, Switzerland* (July 16-25, 1974), identify ourselves in several ways. To begin with, we had come *from more than 150 nations.* TIME magazine referred to the Congress as "a formidable forum, possibly the widest-ranging meeting of Christians ever held." Across the wall behind the platform the Congress slogan was displayed in the six official languages: "Let the Earth Hear His Voice." Yet we were made aware that the earth had already begun to hear and respond, for the 2,700 participants, with the whole spectrum of skin pigmentation and colorful costumes, seemed to have come from every corner of the globe. It was a special joy that 50 percent of the participants, and also of the speakers and the Planning Committee, were from the Third World. One major sorrow was that a few countries, including the USSR and mainland China, were unrepresented.

Despite the diversity of our racial and cultural backgrounds, however, we were conscious of a deep and wonderful unity. For we were all *members of the Church of Jesus Christ,* Christians who take both Christ and Church seriously. We do not confuse the two, imagining that to belong to the visible church necessarily implies that we also belong to Jesus Christ. On the other hand, we acknowledge that we cannot call Jesus Lord and not be responsible members of his new community. In particular, as evangelical Christians, we *praise God for his great salvation* which he has once for all achieved and now bestows through Jesus Christ.

Aware of our common share in this salvation, we *rejoice in the fellowship he has given us with himself and with each other.*

3

b. The Lausanne spirit

It is always difficult to express a mood in words. Yet "the spirit of Lausanne" was more tangible than are most spirits. Its first element comes out in the phrase *we are deeply stirred by what God is doing in our day.* For we are convinced that he is on the move, and we have been excited by the evidence laid before us in stories and statistics. Secondly, we are *moved to penitence by our failures.* Several speakers voiced the hope that the Congress would be marked more by evangelical penitence than by evangelical triumphalism. "Triumphalism" is an attitude of self-confidence and self-congratulation, which is never appropriate in God's children. But the spirit of Lausanne was a spirit of humility and a spirit of penitence. Thirdly, a sense of our past failures and of God's present action leads inevitably to a purposeful look into the future: we are *challenged by the unfinished task of evangelization,* and the challenge has not fallen on deaf ears.

c. The Lausanne Covenant

It is, then, such people in such a spirit, who felt the need to bind themselves together in a commitment or "covenant." *We believe the Gospel is God's good news for the whole world.* Does this talk of world conquest sound presumptuous? If it is, we are content to bear the criticism, for Christians are ambassadors for Jesus Christ, and the world empire we seek (as Jesus told us to, Matt. 6: 33) is the kingdom of God. So *we are determined by his grace to obey Christ's commission.* The reference is to the "great" or "universal" commission of the risen Lord, which was both to *proclaim* the Gospel *to all mankind* ("the whole creation," Mark 16:15) and *to make disciples of every nation (Matt. 28:19).*

We desire, therefore, to affirm our faith (our belief that the Gospel is God's good news for the world) *and our resolve* (our determination to proclaim it to all mankind), and in the light of these things not just to enter into a private commitment ourselves but *to make public our covenant.*

4

*We affirm our belief in the one-eternal God, Creator and
Lord of the world, Father, Son and Holy Spirit, who
governs all things according to the purpose of his will. He
has been calling out from the world a people for himself,
and sending his people back into the world to be his servants and his witnesses, for the extension of his kingdom,
the building up of Christ's body, and the glory of his
name. We confess with shame that we have often denied
our calling and failed in our mission, by becoming conformed to the world or by withdrawing from it. Yet we
rejoice that even when borne by earthen vessels the Gospel is still a precious treasure. To the task of making that
treasure known in the power of the Holy Spirit we desire
to dedicate ourselves anew.*

The Covenant opens with a paragraph about God because
God is the beginning of all things. However far back we
are able to trace causes and effects, we cannot go further
back than God himself. He is the first cause. So Christians want to think theologically, that is, to relate all
their thinking to God who is the ultimate personal Reality behind everything.

In particular, we cannot talk about mission or evangelism
without first talking about God. For mission and evangelism are not the novel ideas of modern men, but part
of the eternal purpose of God. The paragraph refers
briefly to who God is and what he does, goes on to describe his plan for his people, and ends with an assurance
of his power even in our human weakness.

a. The Being of God

No attempt is made to give a full statement of biblical
teaching about God. We affirm our belief in God and
concentrate on a few essentials of our faith in him. It
may be helpful to consider these in pairs.

First, God is both eternal and active in time. He is *the
. . . eternal God,* existing outside time and before time
began. Scripture is clear about this. "From everlasting to
everlasting thou art God" (Psa. 90:2). Nevertheless (to
use the terms of classical theology) the God who is
"transcendent" beyond the universe is also "immanent"
within it. He brought it into being and rules all that he
has made. He is *Creator and Lord of the world.* The two

5

truths are brought together in Isaiah 40:28, "The LORD is the everlasting God, the Creator of the ends of the earth."

Secondly, God is both one and three. He is *the one . . . God . . ., Father, Son and Holy Spirit.* There can be no question of his unity. The Christian affirms this as strongly as any Jew or Muslim. "The LORD our God is one LORD" (Deut. 6:4). He says, "I am the LORD, and there is no other, beside me there is no God (Isa. 45:5). The unity of the Godhead is fundamental to all evangelism. It is because "there is one God" that he demands and deserves the total allegiance of all mankind (Deut. 6: 4,5; Mark 12:29,30; I Tim. 2:5). Yet this one God revealed himself in three stages (first as the God of Israel, then as the incarnate Lord, then as the Holy Spirit) in such a way as to show that he exists eternally in these three personal modes of being. So the risen Jesus has commanded us to baptize converts "in the name (note the singular) of the Father and of the Son and of the Holy Spirit" (Matt. 28:19).

Thirdly, God rules both nature and history. He who is the *Creator and Lord of the world* also *governs all things according to the purpose of his will.* So convinced of this were the apostles that they believed even the hostility of persecutors to be under the control of God. Forbidden to preach, and threatened with severe penalties if they disobeyed, they cried to God as "Sovereign Lord" and declared that the opposition of men to Christ was part of his predestinating plan (Acts 4:28). This must be so, because God "accomplishes all things according to the counsel of his will" (Eph. 1:11).

b. The Purpose of God

From the work of God as Lord of nature and history, the Covenant turns to his redeeming purpose, namely to call out *a people for himself.* It began with Abraham, to whom God said, "I will make of you a great nation . . . and by you all the families of the earth shall bless themselves" (Gen. 12:1-3). It continued with Israel, with whom after the Exodus God renewed his covenant of grace, "You shall be my own possession among all peoples" (Ex. 19:3-6). It is now finding its completion

6

(through the evangelistic work of the church) in the inclusion of Gentile believers, "God . . . visited the Gentiles, to take out of them a people for his name" (Acts 15:14), until in the end there will gather before God's throne a countless, international throng and his promise to Abraham will be finally fulfilled (Rev. 7:9). This concept of the church as a "people for God's possession" is taken up in the New Testament (e.g., I Pet. 2:9) and indicates that worship is the church's first vocation.

The Lausanne Covenant, in speaking of the people of God, concentrates on the relation of the church to the world, that is, of Christian people to non-Christian people or to secular society. It brings together two complementary aspects of this relation: *He has been calling out from the world a people for himself, and sending his people back into the world.* Jesus himself referred to this double role of the church in his prayer recorded in John 17. He began by describing his own as "the men whom thou gavest me out of the world" (vv. 6,9). Yet those who in one sense had been taken "out of" the world in another sense had not, for they were still in it. Jesus could go on to say, "I am no more in the world, but they are in the world" (v. 11). Moreover, it was not enough for them to reside "in" the world; he had to send them "into" the world (v. 18). These prepositions "out of," "in" and "into" together portray what the Christian's relation to the unbelieving world should be.

When we talk about the church being "sent into the world" we are talking about its mission, for that is what the word means. And what is the church's mission in the world? Evangelism yes, but not that alone. For God sends his people out *to be his servants and his witnesses.* Not one or the other, but both. Jesus came to serve (Mark 10:45) and he came to witness (John 18:37). The same two activities constitute the church's mission. They are elaborated later in the Covenant, evangelism in paragraph 4 and Christian social responsibility in paragraph 5. Meanwhile, the objectives of the church's mission are outlined as *the extension of his kingdom* (which Jesus talked about so much, e.g., Matt. 6:10,33; 13:31,32), *the building up of Christ's body* (which Paul wrote about, e.g., Eph. 4:11-16) and *the glory of his name* (which is not only the ultimate aim of mission but also "the chief end of man," cf., Psa. 115:1; Eph. 1:6,12,14).

This affirmation about God and his high purpose for the church in the world inevitably leads us to *confess with shame that we have often denied our calling and failed in our mission.* For we often tend to go to one or the other of two opposite extremes. Either we are so determined to live in the world and maintain contact with non-Christians that we begin to assimilate non-Christian ideas and standards, and are then guilty of *becoming conformed to the world* (Rom. 12:1,2); or we are so determined not to lose our distinctive Christian identity that we begin to shun contact with non-Christians in the world, and then become guilty of *withdrawing from it* (John 17:15; I Cor. 5:10). The best way to avoid these two mistakes of conformity and withdrawal is to be engaged in mission. For if we remember that we are sent into the world as Christ's representatives, we can neither conform to it or we cease to represent him, nor withdraw from it or we have no one to represent him to.

c. The Power of God

The consciousness of our failures can be no excuse for opting out of our responsibilities. It is true that we are like *earthen vessels* — frail, weak and fragile. But these vessels carry *a precious treasure, the Gospel,* and it is through our very weakness that the power of God is best exhibited (II Cor. 4:7; cf., I Cor. 2:3-5 and II Cor. 12: 9,10). So the Covenant's first paragraph ends with a reference (expanded in paragraph 14) to *the power of the Holy Spirit* for the evangelistic task to which *we desire to dedicate ourselves anew.*

Questions for study:

1. What is the importance of the doctrine of God in connection with evangelism?

2. Read John 17:9-19 and summarize from Christ's teaching there the Christian's relation to the world.

8

3. Would the attitude of your local church to the world be most accurately described as one of "conformity," "withdrawal" or "mission"? What steps could be taken to remedy whatever you may find to be wrong?

THE AUTHORITY AND POWER OF THE BIBLE *We affirm the divine inspiration, truthfulness and authority of both Old and New Testament Scriptures in their entirety as the only written Word of God, without error in all that it affirms, and the only infallible rule of faith and practice. We also affirm the power of God's Word to accomplish his purpose of salvation. The message of the Bible is addressed to all mankind. For God's revelation in Christ and in Scripture is unchangeable. Through it the Holy Spirit still speaks today. He illumines the minds of God's people in every culture to perceive its truth freshly through their own eyes and thus discloses to the whole church ever more of the many-colored wisdom of God.*

It may seem strange that the Lausanne Covenant, which is primarily concerned with worldwide evangelization, should include a statement about biblical authority and indeed emphasize it by putting it in such a prominent place, second only to the doctrine of God. But this faithfully reflects the Congress program in which the first Biblical Foundation Paper was entitled "Biblical Authority and Evangelism." Dr. Susumu Uda began, "The problem of authority is the most fundamental problem that the Christian Church always faces." Both evangelism and the nurture of converts involve teaching and therefore raise the question, "What shall we teach?" As Dr. Francis Schaeffer wrote in his later paper, "The Gospel we preach must be rich in content." And this content must be biblical content. The Covenant concentrates on three features of the Bible — its authority, its power and its interpretation.

a. The Authority of the Bible

What is meant by "the Bible" is *both Old and New Testament Scriptures in their entirety*, and these are described as *the only written Word of God.* Scripture is "the Word of God" because God "spoke" it (Heb. 1:1,2; I Thess. 2:13); it is his "written Word" for he then caused it to be recorded for the instruction of later generations (Rom. 15:4; I Cor. 10:6,11; I Tim. 3:14,15); and it is his "only" written Word, for we cannot accept the so-called sacred scriptures of other religions (e.g., the Koran or the Book of Mormon) as having come out of the mind and mouth of God. Three words are used to define more clearly the divine origin of

Scripture - *inspiration, truthfulness* and *authority.*

(i.) *Inspiration.* This does not mean that God somehow breathed into words which had already been written, or into the writers who wrote them, but rather that the words themselves were "God-breathed" (II Tim. 3:16, literally). Of course, they were also the words of men who spoke and wrote freely. Yet these men were "moved by the Holy Spirit" (II Pet. 1:21) to such an extent that it could be said of their words "the mouth of the Lord has spoken it" (Isa. 40:5).

(ii.) *Truthfulness.* Since Scripture is God's Word written, it is of course true. For "God is not man that he should lie" (Num. 23:19). On the contrary, as Jesus himself said in prayer to the Father, "Thy word is truth" (John 17:17). And since it is true, it is *without error in all that it affirms.* Notice the careful qualification. For not everything contained in Scripture is affirmed by Scripture. To take an extreme example, Psalm 14:1 contains the statement "there is no God." This statement is false. But then Scripture is not affirming it. What Scripture affirms in that verse is not atheism, but the folly of atheism, "The fool says in his heart, 'There is no God'." It is important, therefore, in all our Bible study to consider the intention of the author, and what is being asserted. It is this, whatever the subject of the assertion may be, which is true, true and inerrant.

(iii.) *Authority.* The order of the three words is logical. It is the divine *inspiration* of Scripture which has secured its *truthfulness,* and it is because Scripture is truth from God that it has *authority* over men. Indeed (echoing the Westminster Confession) it is *the only infallible rule of faith and practice.* Different churches value secondary rules (creeds, confessions and traditions) to govern their faith (what they believe and teach) and their practice (what they do), but Scripture is the only infallible rule, to whose authority therefore all churches should humbly bow. Jesus himself, in his controversy with the Pharisees, made it plain that ecclesiastical traditions must always be subservient to Scripture, because the former are man's words, while the latter is God's (Mark 7:1-13). Indeed, Jesus' own reverent submission to the Old Testament Scriptures and his provision for the New Testament Scriptures by his appointment of the apostles are together one of the principal reasons for our own acceptance of the authority of Scripture. The disciple is not above his master.

b. The Power of the Bible

We also affirm the power of God's Word to accomplish his purpose . . . God's words are not like our words. Human words are often as feeble as the breath with which they are spoken. But when God speaks he acts. His Word never returns to him empty, but always accomplishes his purpose (Isa. 55:11). For example, it was by his Word that he created, "God said . . . and it was so" (Gen. 1:9, and throughout the chapter). "He spoke, and it came to be" (Psa. 33:6,9).

What is true of creation is equally true of *his purpose of salvation.* The Gospel itself is "the power of God for salvation to everyone who has faith" (Rom. 1:16). Man cannot save himself by his own wisdom. Instead, it pleases God "through the folly of what we preach to save those who believe" (I Cor. 1:21). Not that we should separate the power of God's Word from the power of God's Spirit. The Spirit uses the Word, and speaks and acts through it (e.g., I Cor. 2:1-5; I Thess. 1:5; I Pet. 1:12). Scripture is rich in the metaphors with which it indicates the power of the Word in the hand of the Spirit (e.g., Jer. 23:29 "fire" and "hammer"; Eph. 6:17 and Heb. 4:12 "sword"; I Pet. 1:23 and Jas. 1:21 "seed," etc.). This assurance should give great confidence to all Christians who in their preaching and witnessing handle Scripture faithfully and humbly.

c. The Interpretation of the Bible

The last four sentences of the paragraph touch upon an important paradox regarding our understanding of God's Word.

On the one hand, *the message of the Bible* is exactly the same for all men in all places and at all times. Its relevance is not limited to any particular generation or any particular culture. On the contrary, it is *addressed to all mankind.* This is because *God's revelation in Christ and in Scripture is unchangeable.* As Jesus said, it "cannot be broken" (John 10:35, cf. Matt. 5:17,18). It has been delivered to us "once for all" unalterably (Jude 3). And being God's truth it possesses a marvelous universality. As *through it the Holy Spirit still speaks today*, it has a message for everybody everywhere.

On the other hand, its unalterability is not a dead, wooden, colorless uniformity. For as the Holy Spirit used the personality and culture of the writers of his Word in order to convey through each something fresh and appropriate, so today *he illumines the minds of God's people in every culture to perceive its truth freshly through their own eyes*. It is he who opens the eyes of our hearts (Eph. 1:17, 18), and these eyes and hearts belong to young and old, Latin and Anglo-Saxon, African, Asian and American, male and female, poetic and prosaic. It is this "magnificent and intricate mosaic of mankind" (to borrow a phrase of Dr. Donald McGavran's) which the Holy Spirit uses to disclose from Scripture *ever more of the many-colored wisdom of God* (a literal translation of Eph. 3:10). Thus *the whole church* is needed to receive God's whole revelation in all its beauty and richness (cf., Eph. 3:18 "with all the saints").

Questions for study:

1. What relevance to evangelism has the Covenant's strong assertion of the inspiration and authority of the Bible?

2. What difference will it make to our evangelism if we really believe that God's Word has power?

3. The Covenant draws a distinction between the Holy Spirit's work in "revelation" (the writing of the Bible) and his work in "illumination" (the reading of the Bible). Why is this important?

THE UNIQUENESS AND UNIVERSALITY OF CHRIST *We affirm that there is only one Savior and only one Gospel, although there is a wide diversity of evangelistic approaches. We recognize that all men have some knowledge of God through his general revelation in nature. But we deny that this can save, for men suppress the truth by their unrighteousness. We also reject as derogatory to Christ and the Gospel every kind of syncretism and dialogue which implies that Christ speaks equally through all religions and ideologies. Jesus Christ, being himself the only God-man, who gave himself as the only ransom for sinners, is the only mediator between God and man. There is no other name by which we must be saved. All men are perishing because of sin, but God loves all men, not wishing that any should perish but that all should repent. Yet those who reject Christ repudiate the joy of salvation and condemn themselves to eternal separation from God. To proclaim Jesus as "the Savior of the world" is not to affirm that all men are either automatically or ultimately saved, still less to affirm that all religions offer salvation in Christ. Rather it is to proclaim God's love for a world of sinners and to invite all men to respond to him as Savior and Lord in the wholehearted personal commitment of repentance and faith. Jesus Christ has been exalted above every other name; we long for the day when every knee shall bow to him and every tongue shall confess him Lord.*

This section opens with the strong affirmation that *there is only one Savior and only one Gospel.* Some modern theologians try to prove that even the New Testament itself contains a multiplicity of contradictory gospels. Strange! They cannot have grasped Paul's assertion about the unity of the apostolic message (I Cor. 15:11; NB, the pronouns "I," "they," "we" and "you"), or felt the vehemence with which he anathematizes anybody (including even himself, and even an angel from heaven) who "should preach . . . a gospel contrary to that which we preached to you . . . contrary to that which you received" (Gal. 1:6-9). Professor Henri Blocher rightly emphasized at Lausanne that what we have in the New Testament is "diversity without conflict"; not contradictions but "an unartificial harmony of teachings given so diversely" as to indicate its divine origin.

At the same time, the Covenant immediately guards itself against two misunderstandings. When we assert that there is only one Gospel we are asserting the uniqueness of its content, and neither that there is only one way of presenting it nor that those ignorant of it have no knowledge of truth at all. As to the former, *there is a wide diversity of evangelistic approaches.* Canon Michael Green expressed this well in reference to Paul, "Great flexibility in presentation, but great firmness on content was his emphasis." And Dr. George Peters in his wide survey entitled "Contemporary Practices of Evangelism" emphasized the virtues of "flexibility, variability and openness."

What, then, about those ignorant of the Gospel? Are we to say that they are ignorant of God altogether, including those who adhere to non-Christian religions? No. *We recognize that all men have some knowledge of God.* This universal (though partial) knowledge is due to his self-revelation, what theologians call *his general revelation* because it is made to all men, or his "natural" revelation because it is made *in nature,* both externally in the universe (Rom. 1:19-21) and internally in the human conscience (Rom. 1:32 and 2:14,15). Such knowledge of God is not saving knowledge, however. *We deny that this can save,* partly because it is a revelation of God's power, deity and holiness (Rom. 1:20,32) but not of his love for sinners or of his plan of salvation, and partly because men do not live up to the knowledge they have. On the contrary, they *suppress the truth by their unrighteousness* (Rom. 1:18), and their rejection of the truth which they know then leads to idolatry, to immorality and to the judgment of God (Rom. 1:21-32). So, far from saving them, their knowledge actually condemns them. And they are without excuse (Rom. 1:20). Therefore, it is false to suppose that sinners can be saved through other systems, or that *Christ speaks equally through all religions and ideologies.* We firmly repudiate *every kind of syncretism and dialogue* which suggests this as *derogatory to Christ and the Gospel.* For these are unique, and non-Christian religions know nothing of them.

a. The Uniqueness of Christ: he is the only Savior

The paragraph goes on to define and defend its opening statement that "there is only one Savior." It relies first on I Tim. 2:5,6: ". . . there is one mediator between God and men, the man Christ Jesus, who gave himself as a ransom for all . . . .." Notice the three nouns which are applied in these verses to Jesus — "mediator," "man" and "ransom." "Man" alludes to his birth of a human mother and "ransom" to his death on the Cross bearing instead of us the penalty we deserved. Or, theologically speaking, these two words refer to his incarnation and his atonement. Both are unique. Neither has any parallel in other religions. And it is precisely because Jesus Christ is *the only God-man* and *the only ransom for sinners* that he is *the only mediator between God and man.* For nobody else possesses his qualifications or even remotely approaches his competence (on account of his divine — human person and atoning death) to save sinners. Further, with this statement of the apostle Paul the apostle Peter was in complete agreement. He said, "There is salvation in no one else, for *there is no other name* under heaven given among men *by which we must be saved"* (Acts 4: 12).

Such a salvation (a rescue, that is, from the guilt of sin and from the judgment of God upon it) is urgently needed because *all men are perishing because of sin.* "Perishing" is a terrible word, but Jesus himself used it (e.g., Matt. 18:14; Luke 13:3,5,cf., John 3:15,16) and so did the apostles (e.g., I Cor. 1:18); therefore we must not shy away from it. *All men* are in this plight until and unless they are saved by Christ. Yet there is something else we know about all men, namely that *God loves all men.* And because of his great love Scripture says that he is forbearing and patient towards sinners, *not wishing that any should perish, but that all should repent* (II Pet. 3:9). Although this is the wish of God (for he says, "I have no pleasure in the death of any one," Ezek. 18:32), we have to add that some will refuse to repent and believe, will instead *reject Christ,* and so will *repudiate the joy of salvation and condemn themselves to eternal separation from God* (cf., II Thess. 1:7-9). The prospect is almost too dreadful to contemplate; we should be able to speak of hell only with tears. Some may ask how these sentences of the Covenant relate to the doctrine of election (which Scripture teaches), and how divine sovereignty in salvation can be reconciled with human responsibility. Theologians have wrestled with this question for centuries. But it should be sufficient for us to accept that the Bible teaches both truths. We could sum it up, however paradoxical it may sound, by saying that those who are saved will ascribe all the credit to God, while those who are lost will accept all the blame themselves.

b. The Universality of Christ:
he is the Savior of the world

In the last sentences of this section the subject moves from the uniqueness of Christ to the universality of Christ. Each truth involves the other. It is because Jesus Christ is the only Savior that he must be universally proclaimed. Many Samaritans called him "the Savior of the world" (John 4:42), and John wrote that "the Father has sent his Son as the Savior of the world" (I John 4:14). So we too may apply this great and glorious title to Jesus. But we must also be clear what we mean by it.

Negatively, we mean neither *that all men are . . . automatically . . . saved* (for men must believe in the Lord Jesus in order to be saved, Acts 16:31) nor that *all men are . . . . ultimately saved* for, alas, some will reject Christ and perish). *Still less* do we mean *that all religions offer salvation in Christ,* because plainly they do not. All non-Christian religions, if they teach salvation at all, offer it only as a reward for merit which has been accumulated by good works, whereas the Christian message is "the Gospel of the grace of God" (Acts 20:24), that is, Good News of his mercy to sinners who deserve nothing at his hand except judgment.

Positively, to proclaim Jesus Christ as "the Savior of the world" is *to proclaim God's love for a world of sinners,* a love so great that he gave his only Son even to the death of the Cross (John 3:16; Rom. 5:8; I John 4:9,10). It is also *to invite all men to respond to him,* for the Gospel must be shared with men without any distinction whatsoever. Perhaps nobody in history has had a clearer understanding or heavier burden regarding the universality of the Gospel than the apostle Paul. It weighed upon him as a debt he must discharge. "I am under obligation," he wrote "both to Greeks and to barbarians, both to the wise and to the foolish" (Rom. 1:14). That is, neither racial nor social barriers must be raised against the preaching of the Gospel. In particular, the same Gospel must be made known to both Jews and Gentiles, or more accurately "to the Jew first and also to the Greek" (e.g., Rom. 1:16; 10:12). Some of our Jewish brothers were understandably disappointed that the Covenant contained no reference to them. And with the benefit of hindsight we can now apologize. For God has by no means rejected his ancient people (Rom. 11:1,2), but on the contrary still purposes "their full inclusion" (Rom. 11:12 ff.). So the invitation goes out to Jew and Gentile alike to *respond* to Christ *as Savior and Lord in the wholehearted personal commitment of repentance and faith.* Paul called it "the obedience of faith" (Rom. 1: 5; 16:26). More is said about this in the next paragraph. The essential fact is that *Jesus Christ has been exalted above every other name,* for God has given him the supreme place at his own right hand, "far above" every other conceivable competitor (Eph. 1:20-23; Phil. 2:9). God's purpose in thus exalting Jesus was and is "that at the name of Jesus every knee should bow . . . and every tongue confess that Jesus Christ is Lord . . ." (Phil. 2: 10,11). We too should long that the lordship of Jesus Christ should be acknowledged. There is no greater incentive to evangelism than this. Moreover, we know that in the end every knee will be obliged to bow to Christ, for even his enemies will "be made a stool for his feet" (Heb. 10:12,13; cf., Psa. 110:1). And because our eyes have been opened to see the supremacy of Jesus Christ, *we long for the day when every knee shall bow to him,* some voluntarily, others involuntarily, *and every tongue shall confess him Lord.*

Questions for study:

1. "Comparative religion" is a popular study today; wherein lies the uniqueness of Christianity?

2. What light does this paragraph throw on the condition of non-Christians?

3. It is sometimes said that we have no right to interfere in another person's religion. How does this paragraph help you to reply?

THE NATURE OF EVANGELISM

To evangelize is to spread the good news that Jesus Christ died for our sins and was raised from the dead according to the Scriptures, and that as the reigning Lord he now offers the forgiveness of sins and the liberating gift of the Spirit to all who repent and believe. Our Christian presence in the world is indispensable to evangelism, and so is that kind of dialogue whose purpose is to listen sensitively in order to understand. But evangelism itself is the proclamation of the historical, biblical Christ as Savior and Lord, with a view to persuading people to come to him personally and so be reconciled to God. In issuing the Gospel invitation we have no liberty to conceal the cost of discipleship. Jesus still calls all who would follow him to deny themselves, take up their cross, and identify themselves with his new community. The results of evangelism include obedience to Christ, incorporation into his church and responsible service in the world.

In his opening address at Lausanne, Dr. Billy Graham expressed as his first hope for the Congress that it would "frame a biblical declaration on evangelism," and in his final address he declared himself satisfied that it had done so. The fourth paragraph of the Covenant begins with a definition, and goes on to describe the context of evangelism, namely what must precede and follow it.

a. The Definition of Evangelism

The English word "evangelism" is derived from a Greek term meaning literally "to bring or to spread good news." It is impossible, therefore, to talk about evangelism without talking about the content of the good news. What is it? At its very simplest, it is *Jesus*. Jesus Christ himself is the essence of the Gospel. If we were to transliterate Acts 8:35, we would say that Philip "evangelized to him Jesus," that is, he told him the good news of Jesus (cf., Rom. 1:1,3). But what *is* the good news of Jesus? The Covenant statement attempts to summarize it as it was expounded by the apostle Peter in his early speeches in the Acts (especially 2:22-39) and by the apostle Paul in I Cor. 15:1 ff.

The first element is those two pivotal events, the death and resurrection of Jesus. The apostles also alluded to his birth and life, his words and works, his reign and return, but they concentrated on *the good news that Jesus Christ died for our sins and was raised from the dead.* His death and resurrection were to them verifiable historical events. And they were significant events, for Christ died *for our sins,* to bear their condemnation and secure our justification, and he *was raised* to prove that his sacrifice for sin had been accepted and that he had not died in vain (Rom. 4:25; I Cor. 15:17-19).

The second element in the early apostolic preaching of the Gospel concerned the witnesses to these events, namely the Old Testament prophets and the apostles' own eyewitness experience. Consequently they kept quoting from the Old Testament and kept adding "we are witnesses of these things." In brief, they preached the death and resurrection of Jesus Christ *according to the Scriptures* (I Cor. 15:3,4). Among several popular re-interpretations of Jesus today are Jesus the violent revolutionary, Jesus the circus clown (of *Godspell*), and Jesus the disillusioned superstar. Over against these fantasies of men's minds we must be faithful to the authentic Jesus, who is *the historical, biblical Christ* (as he is described in the middle of this section), Jesus Christ according to the Scriptures of both Old and New Testaments.

Thirdly, the Good News relates not only to what Christ once did (when he died and was raised from death) but to what he *now offers.* For he is now exalted to God's right hand, and from that position of unique authority as *the reigning Lord* he promises to penitent believers two most marvelous gifts: *the forgiveness of sins* (remitting our guilt and instating us in the favor and the family of God), and *the liberating gift of the Spirit* (for the Holy Spirit is given to all who come to Christ, and the Spirit sets us free from self-centeredness to live for God and for others).

Fourthly, in order to receive these free gifts men must *repent and believe,* turning from their sins, lies and idols (repentance) and trusting in Jesus Christ as the only Savior (faith). The two belong together, for "faith without repentance is not saving faith but presumptuous believism" (Dr. René Padilla). Perhaps baptism should also be montioned here, for this is where the apostles put it (e.g., Acts 2:38). Since it is administered "in the name of Jesus Christ" it at least signifies publicly a penitent faith in the very Lord Jesus who had previously been repudiated.

Here, then, is the irreducible minimum of the apostolic Gospel. We must never stray from these events and their witnesses, from the offer that is based upon the events, or from the conditions on which the offer depends.

b. The Prelude to Evangelism

True evangelism can never take place in a vacuum. It presupposes a context from which it must not be isolated. A certain situation precedes it; certain consequences follow it. In referring to this, the Covenant deliberately uses the words presence, proclamation, persuasion, and dialogue which have all figured prominently in recent theological debate. In essence, it insists that *evangelism . . . is the proclamation of the historical, biblical Christ as Savior and Lord.* For the only Jesus there is to proclaim is the Jesus of history, who is the Jesus of Scripture, who is "our Lord and Savior Jesus Christ" (e.g., II Pet. 3:18). So we have no liberty to preach his salvation without his lordship, or his lordship without his salvation. Listen to Paul, "We preach Christ crucified" (I Cor. 1:23) and "we preach . . . Jesus Christ as Lord" (II Cor. 4:5).

Yet the prelude to proclamation is presence. For how can we share Christ with people with whom we have no contact? Hence *our Christian presence in the world is indispensable to evangelism.* The first word of Jesus' Great Commission was not "preach" but "go." For we cannot proclaim Christ from a distance, but only to people to whom we have gone and with whom we have sought to identify. So *presence* is not a substitute for *proclamation* (as some maintain), but rather an indispensable prelude to it. It is in this situation that *dialogue* with non-Christians is not only right but is also (like *presence*) indispensable. *Dialogue* is a much misused word. Some people are using it to describe a situation of compromise in which the Christian renounces his own Christian commitment and regards the Gospel as open to debate! *That kind of dialogue we have already rejected (in paragraph 3) as "derogatory to Christ and the Gospel." But, properly defined, a dialogue is a conversation in which both parties are serious, and each is prepared to listen to the other. Its *purpose is to listen sensitively in order to understand.* Such listening is an essential prelude to evangelism, for how can we share the Good News relevantly if we do not understand the other person's position and problems?

c. The Consequences of Evangelism

Although evangelism is itself the spreading of the Good News, it is not unconcerned about people's response to the message they hear. On the contrary, evangelism is proclamation with a view to persuasion. The World Congress on Evangelism at Berlin in 1966 declared that "evangelism is the proclamation of the Gospel . . . with the purpose of persuading condemned and lost sinners to put their trust in God . . . " The Lausanne Covenant similarly asserts that evangelism is the proclamation of Christ *with a view to persuading people to come to him personally and so be reconciled to God.* There can be no doubt that *persuading* figured prominently in the early church's evangelism. Paul summed up his ministry by saying "we persuade men" (II Cor. 5:11); and in the Acts, Luke describes him doing it (e.g., 17:1-4; 18:4; 19:8-10, 26; 28: 23,24). Clearly, the apostles did not regard the use of argument as incompatible with trust in the Holy Spirit. We too must not be afraid to expound and argue the Gospel today.

This work of persuasion must be honest and open. We have nothing to hide. For example, *in issuing the Gospel invitation we have no liberty to conceal the cost of discipleship.* Jesus himself, far from concealing anything, urged his would-be followers before committing themselves to him to "sit down first and count the cost" (Luke 14:28,31). He laid down in the plainest terms the conditions a person must fulfill, without which "he cannot be my disciple" (Luke 14:26,27,33). And *Jesus still calls all who would follow him* today, just as he did during his public ministry, *to deny themselves* (putting him before self), *take up their cross* (following him to the place of execution, where self is crucified) *and identify themselves with his new community* (Mark 8:34-38).

The objective of evangelism is conversion, and conversion implies a radical change of life-style. It involves the convert in at least three new and conscientious relationships — to Christ, to the church, and to the world. For *the results of evangelism include obedience to Christ* (who is now acknowledged as Lord), *incorporation into his church* (for to belong to Christ is to belong to the people of Christ, Acts 2:40,47), *and responsible service in the world* (for conversion means nothing if it does not result in a change from self-centered living to sacrificial service, Mark 10:43-45).

Questions for study:

1. Using this paragraph as a starting point, summarize (from the New Testament but in your own words) what the Good News is.

2. Compare the references to "dialogue" in paragraph 3 and paragraph 4. What is right and what is wrong about dialogue? Does the right type have a place in your witness?

3. Think of some ways in which you (and your church) could be more faithful in facing people with the cost of discipleship.

4. How would you define the goal of evangelism? Why do we want people to hear the Good News?

We affirm that God is both the Creator and the Judge of all men. We therefore should share his concern for justice and reconciliation throughout human society and for the liberation of men from every kind of oppression. Because mankind is made in the image of God, every person, regardless of race, religion, color, culture, class, sex or age, has an intrinsic dignity because of which he should be respected and served, not exploited. Here too we express penitence both for our neglect and for having sometimes regarded evangelism and social concern as mutually exclusive. Although reconciliation with man is not reconciliation with God, nor is social action evangelism, nor is political liberation salvation, nevertheless we affirm that evangelism and socio-political involvement are both part of our Christian duty. For both are necessary expressions of our doctrines of God and man, our love for our neighbor and our obedience to Jesus Christ. The message of salvation implies also a message of judgment upon every form of alienation, oppression and discrimination, and we should not be afraid to denounce evil and injustice wherever they exist. When people receive Christ they are born again into his kingdom and must seek not only to exhibit but also to spread its righteousness in the midst of an unrighteous world. The salvation we claim should be transforming us in the totality of our personal and social responsibilities. Faith without works is dead.

In the past, especially perhaps in nineteenth century Britain, evangelical Christians had an outstanding record of social action. In this century, however — partly because of our reaction against the "social gospel" of liberal optimism — we have tended to divorce evangelism from social concern, and to concentrate almost exclusively on the former. It may be helpful, therefore, to begin this exposition of section 5 with a reference to two sentences, one of confession and the other of affirmation, which occur about halfway through it.

First, *we express penitence both for our neglect* of our Christian social responsibility and for our naive polarization in *having sometimes regarded evangelism and social concern as mutually exclusive.* This confession is mildly worded. A large group at Lausanne, concerned to develop a radical Christian discipleship, expressed themselves more strongly, "We must repudiate as demonic the attempt to drive a wedge between evangelism and social action." Secondly, and positively, *we affirm that evangelism and social-political involvement are both part of our Christian duty.* More will be said about this phrase later.

Christian duty arises from Christian doctrine. So this section is not content merely to assert that Christians have social responsibilities: it goes on to outline the four main doctrines out of which our Christian social duty springs, namely the doctrines of God, man, salvation, and the kingdom.

a. The Doctrine of God

It is significant that a paragraph which relates entirely to "Christian social responsibility" should open with an affirmation about God. This is right. For our theology must always govern our conduct. *We affirm that God is both the Creator and the Judge of all men.* Thus the creation and judgment, the beginning and the end of time, are brought together (cf., Acts 17:26,31). Both concern *all men,* for God is not just interested in the church but in the world. He created all men, and all men will have to give an account to him on the day of judgment. *Therefore* (notice the deduction which is drawn from the universality of creation and judgment) we who claim to be God's people should share the breadth of God's concerns. In particular, *we should share his concern for justice and reconciliation throughout human society and for the liberation of men from every kind of oppression* (see Amos 1 and 2). Justice, reconciliation and freedom — these are more and more the object of human quest in today's world. But they were God's will for society long before they became man's quest. For God loves the good and hates the evil wherever these are found (Psa. 7:9,11; 11:4-7; 33:5). It is written of his King in the Old Testament and applied to the Lord Jesus in the New, "You love righteousness and hate wickedness" (Psa. 45:7; Heb. 1:9). The same should be true of us all, "Cease to do evil," God says, "learn to do good; seek justice, correct oppression; defend the fatherless, plead for the widow" (Isa. 1:16,17).

b. The Doctrine of Man

Social responsibility and evangelism are together part of our Christian duty for both are necessary expressions of our doctrines of God and man. Particular reference is made to the great biblical affirmation that *mankind is made in the image of God* (Gen. 1:26,27). It is for this reason that man is unique on earth. There is a similarity between men and animals in that both are God's living creatures dependent on him for their being, but a vast dissimilarity in that man alone is a godlike being with such godlike capacities as rationality, conscience, dominion and love. It is the divine image in man which gives him *an intrinsic dignity* or worth, a worth which belongs to all human beings by creation, *regardless of race, religion, color, culture, class, sex or age.* Similarly, the reason why murder is such a terrible crime is that "God made man in his own image" (Gen. 9:5,6). Because of every person's inherent dignity as a godlike being, he *should be respected and served,* and indeed loved (Lev. 19:18; Luke 6:27,35), *not exploited.* Only when we grasp this foundational biblical doctrine shall we begin to see the evils, for example, of racial discrimination and social prejudice. They are an offence to man's dignity and therefore to the God in whose image man is made. It is not exaggerated to say that to insult man in these ways is to blaspheme God (Jas. 3:9,10).

c. The Doctrine of Salvation

Salvation for many people today is a prohibited word: some are embarrassed by it, others say it is meaningless. Certainly it needs to be interpreted for modern men. So there was a good expectation that the World Council of Churches' Commission on World Mission and Evangelism's Assembly at Bangkok in January '73 entitled *Salvation Today* would produce a fresh definition, faithful to Scripture and relevant to today. But Bangkok disappointed us. Although it included some references to personal salvation, its emphasis was to equate salvation with political and economic liberation. The Lausanne Covenant rejects this, for it is not biblical. *Reconciliation with man is not reconciliation with God, nor is social action evangelism, nor is political liberation salvation. Nevertheless,* it is our duty to be involved in sociopolitical action; that is, both in social action (caring for society's casualties) and in political action (concerned for the structures of society itself). For both active evangelistic and social involvement *are necessary expressions* not only of our doctrines of God and man (as we have seen) but also of *our love for our neighbor and our obedience to Jesus Christ.* Further, although salvation is not to be equated with political liberation, yet *the message of salvation implies also a message of judgment upon every form of alienation, oppression and discrimination.* Salvation is deliverance from evil, and implicit in God's desire to save people from evil is his judgment on the evil from which he saves them. Further, this evil is both individual and social. Since God hates evil and injustice, *we should not be afraid to denounce evil and injustice wherever they exist.*

d. The Doctrine of the Kingdom

Section five ends with a challenge to our personal Christian commitment. Christians claim to have received Christ. But do we always remember that *when people receive Christ they are born again into his kingdom* (John 1:12,13; 3:3,5)? To be a citizen of God's kingdom is to be submissive to his righteous rule. As such, we are under obligation *to exhibit* the righteous standards of the kingdom in our own lives. For Jesus taught in the Sermon on the Mount that members of his kingdom must "hunger and thirst for righteousness" and exhibit a righteousness which exceeds the shallow, formal righteousness of the scribes and Pharisees (Matt. 5:6,20). He also said that we must "seek first God's kingdom and his righteousness" (Matt. 6:33); that is, we must set these things before us as the supreme good to which we devote our lives. We must seek not only the spread of the kingdom itself, nor only to exhibit its righteousness ourselves, *but also to spread its righteousness in the midst of an unrighteous world.* How else can we be "the salt of the earth" (Matt. 5:14)?

The last sentences of this section revert to the terminology of salvation, but we must remember that Jesus drew no distinction between salvation and the kingdom of God (e.g., Mark 10:23-27 and cf., Isa. 52:7). *The salvation we claim* (and Christians do humbly claim to have been saved) *should be transforming us.* "Be transformed," Paul commanded the Romans. "We are being transformed," he declared to the Corinthians, using the same Greek verb (Rom. 12:2; II Cor. 3:18). And this transformation, if genuine, should touch every part of us, indeed *the totality of our personal and social responsibilities.* If not, how can we claim to be saved? For *faith without works is dead* (Jas. 2:20).

Questions for study:

1. The Covenant relates duty to doctrine. Take the biblical doctrine of either God or man, and think out what effect it should have on our social responsibilities.

2. If your local church takes its social responsibility seriously, how will this affect its program?

3. "We should not be afraid to denounce evil and injustice . . ." Discuss the implications of this statement.

4. What has salvation got to do with social action?

EVANGELISM AND THE CHURCH

We affirm that Christ sends his redeemed people into the world as the Father sent him, and that this calls for a similar deep and costly penetration of the world. We need to break out of our ecclesiastical ghettos and permeate non-Christian society. In the church's mission of sacrificial service evangelism is primary. World evangelization requires the whole church to take the whole Gospel to the whole world. The church is at the very center of God's cosmic purpose and is his appointed means of spreading the Gospel. But a church which preaches the Cross must itself be marked by the Cross. It becomes a stumbling block to evangelism when it betrays the Gospel or lacks a living faith in God, a genuine love for people, or scrupulous honesty in all things including promotion and finance. The church is the community of God's people rather than an institution, and must not be identified with any particular culture, social or political system, or human ideology.

We affirm that the church's visible unity in truth is God's purpose. Evangelism also summons us to unity, because our oneness strengthens our witness, just as our disunity undermines our Gospel of reconciliation. We recognize, however, that organizational unity may take many forms and does not necessarily forward evangelism. Yet we who share the same biblical faith should be closely united in fellowship, work and witness. We confess that our testimony has sometimes been marred by sinful individualism and needless duplication. We pledge ourselves to seek a deeper unity in truth, worship, holiness and mission. We urge the development of regional and functional cooperation for the furtherance of the church's mission for strategic planning, for mutual encouragement, and for the sharing of resources and experience.

Already in the first paragraph of the Covenant there is a reference to God's purpose for the church. This is now elaborated in two paragraphs which may be studied together. They allude to the church's mission, integrity and unity.

a. The Mission of the Church

The opening affirmation echoes the prayer and the commission of Jesus (John 17:18; 20:21): *we affirm that*

Christ sends his redeemed people into the world as the Father sent him. It recognizes that Christ's mission in the world is to be the model of the church (NB, the "asso" in both texts), and that *this calls for a similar deep and costly penetration of the world.* For when the Son of God was sent into the world he did not remain aloof from its life or pain. On the contrary, he penetrated deep into our humanity by the incarnation, and by becoming man he became vulnerable to temptation and suffering. Dr. Ralph Winter introduced us at Lausanne to the distinction he draws between three kinds of evangelism — E-1 (within our own culture and language), E-2 (reaching people of a similar culture and language), and E-3 (cross-cultural evangelism). In all three kinds, the Christian must identify with those he is seeking to reach, striving to enter their thought world. But E-3 evangelism is likely to be the most costly because the gulf to be crossed is deeper and wider. All of us *need to break out of our ecclesiastical ghettos and permeate non-Christian society.* This is part and parcel of *the church's mission of sacrificial service.* As we have seen, it includes both evangelistic and social action, so that normally the church will not have to choose between them.

But if a choice has to be made, then *evangelism is primary.* Two reasons are given. The first is the immensity of the task: *world evangelization requires the whole church to take the whole Gospel to the whole world.* Unless the whole church is mobilized, the whole world is not likely to be reached. The second is the biblical truth that the church is not a man-made society but, on the contrary, *is at the very center of God's cosmic purpose.* This phrase comes from the Rev. Howard Snyder's paper entitled "The Church as God's Agent of Evangelism." He adds, "Paul was concerned to speak of the Church as the result of, and within the context of, the plan of God for his whole creation" (Eph. 1:9,10,20-23; 3:10; 6:12). In addition, the church is God's *appointed means of spreading the Gospel.* Thus, God's purpose and the world's need together bring to the church an insistent call to evangelize.

b. The Integrity of the Church

Halfway through paragraph six comes a significant *but*. It introduces the uncomfortable question of the church's credibility. The church may evangelize (preach the Gospel); but will the world hear and heed its message? Not unless the church retains its own integrity, the Covenant insists. If we hope to be listened to, we must practice what we preach. Our behavior must be "worthy of the Gospel" (Phil. 1:27). And not our individual behavior only. For the Gospel is proclaimed by the church. And, as Samuel Escobar insisted in his address at Lausanne, the church must demonstrate that it is a "radically different community," with new standards, a new view of money and property, a new attitude to secular power, and a new power of its own (the Holy Spirit), and an altogether new quality of love and brotherhood.

In particular, the Cross must be as central to our lives as it is to our message. Do we preach Christ crucified (I Cor. 1:23)? Then let us remember that *a church which preaches the Cross must itself be marked by the Cross* (Gal. 6:14,17), that is, by self-denial, self-humbling, and self-giving. This striking reference to the Cross is taken from the *Response to Lausanne* composed by the "radical discipleship" group. They interpret what they mean by adding that the church must "identify and agonize with men, renounce status and demonic power, and give itself in selfless service of others for God." Otherwise the very church which is intended to be the agent of evangelism *becomes a stumbling block to evangelism* (cf., II Cor. 6:3). Four "scandals" (the Greek word for stumbling blocks) are singled out, namely when the church *betrays the Gospel* (distorting its content in any way), *or lacks a living faith in God* (by putting its confidence elsewhere), *a genuine love for people* (by any failure in Christian caring), *or scrupulous honesty in all things — including promotion and finance.* It may well be as evil in God's sight to falsify facts in our statistical reports, or to falsify our accounts, as it is to falsify our message.

It is all the more important for the church to retain its own integrity because of what it is. It is not primarily *an institution;* nor must it be *identified with any particular culture, social or political system, or human ideology.*

The church is above and beyond all these organizations of man. It is *the community of God's people.* It bears God's name and so puts God's name at risk.

c. The Unity of the Church

Paragraph seven broaches the difficult subjects of unity and cooperation. It begins with two reasons why we should be concerned for the unity of the church, the first theological and the second pragmatic. Theologically, *we affirm that the church's visible unity in truth is God's purpose.* Of course, in one sense the church's unity already exists and can no more be destroyed than the unity of the Godhead (Eph. 4:4-6), but this invisible, indestructible unity still needs to become a *visible unity* (Eph. 4:3). It must also be a *unity in truth* (Eph. 4:13). This is the kind of unity for which Jesus prayed. It would come about only through the revelation of the Father which he had given to the apostles (John 17:11,20-23).

The second and pragmatic reason for this quest is that *evangelism . . . summons us to unity.* Our message is one of love and peace, but it always rings hollow when we are not living in love and peace ourselves (John 13:35; 17:21). Therefore, *our oneness strengthens our witness, just as our disunity undermines our Gospel of reconciliation.*

At the same time, we have to admit two facts about *organizational unity.* The first is that *it may take many forms.* For about fifty years following World War I it was generally assumed that "organic union" or the total merger of churches was the right way forward. But now rigid structures are everywhere being questioned, and people are not so sure. Visible unity should certainly be characterized by a common confession of truth, but in other matters by diversity and flexibility. The second fact about organizational unity is that it *does not necessarily forward evangelism.* Leaders of some united churches have admitted with sorrow that union has not brought that impetus to evangelize which they had expected.

Since the only unity pleasing to God is unity in truth, surely *we who share the same biblical faith should be closely united in fellowship, work and witness.* For, though we still disagree with one another on some secondary issues, we stand firm and stand together on the great fundamentals of the biblical revelation. Yet we have to admit our frequent failures in this area. *We confess that our testimony has sometimes been marred by sinful individualism* (we evangelicals are often rugged individualists), and by *needless duplication* (at times we appear to prefer to build our own little empire rather than to allow our distinctive work to be absorbed in common action for the common good). After this statement of what we ought to be (closely united) and this confession of what we sometimes are (sinful individualists), the paragraph ends with a pledge and a plea.

First, *we pledge ourselves to seek a deeper unity in truth, worship, holiness and mission.* That is, we who are one in truth undertake by God's grace to seek to worship God together, to grow together in Christ-likeness, and together to share in the mission of the church. Then the plea: *we urge the development of regional and functional cooperation.* A questionnaire was submitted to the Lausanne Congress participants, asking whether they would favor any kind of post-Congress organization. In reply, quite strong opposition was expressed to the notion of a centralized evangelical world structure, but a comparably strong desire was voiced for evangelical cooperation regionally and functionally. The Lausanne Continuation Committee, which has been formed from names chosen by Congress participants, will seek to implement this desire, and will no doubt bear in mind the purposes of cooperation with which this paragraph of the Covenant concludes, namely *for the furtherance of the church's mission, for strategic planning, for mutual encouragement, and for the sharing of resources and experience.* In other words, we must learn to plan and work together, and also to give to one another and receive from one another whatever good gifts God has given us.

Questions for study:

1. *Penetrate* and *permeate* are two verbs used in paragraph six to describe the church's mission. What will this mean in practice?

2. The second part of paragraph six is outspoken in saying what makes the church a stumbling block to evangelism. Examine your life and your church's life in the light of this analysis.

3. Paragraph seven is about unity and cooperation. Can you apply it to your local situation?

PARTNERSHIP IN WORLD EVANGELIZATION

We rejoice that a new missionary era has dawned. The dominant role of western missions is fast disappearing. God is raising up from the younger churches a great new resource for world evangelization, and is thus demonstrating that the responsibility to evangelize belongs to the whole body of Christ. All churches should therefore be asking God and themselves what they should be doing both to reach their own area and to send missionaries to other parts of the world. A re-evaluation of our missionary responsibility and role should be continuous. Thus a growing partnership of churches will develop and the universal character of Christ's church will be more clearly exhibited. We also thank God for agencies which labor in Bible translation, theological education, the mass media, Christian literature, evangelism, missions, church renewal and other specialist fields. They too should engage in constant self-examination to evaluate their effectiveness as part of the church's mission.

More than 2,700 million people, which is more than two-thirds of mankind, have yet to be evangelized. We are ashamed that so many have been neglected; it is a standing rebuke to us and to the whole church. There is now, however, in many parts of the world an unprecedented receptivity to the Lord Jesus Christ. We are convinced that this is the time for churches and para-church agencies to pray earnestly for the salvation of the unreached and to launch new efforts to achieve world evangelization. A reduction of foreign missionaries and money in an evangelized country may sometimes be necessary to facilitate the national church's growth in self-reliance and to release resources for unevangelized areas. Missionaries should flow ever more freely from and to all six continents in a spirit of humble service. The goal should be, by all available means and at the earliest possible time, that every person will have the opportunity to hear, understand, and receive the good news. We cannot hope to attain this goal without sacrifice. All of us are shocked by the poverty of millions and disturbed by the injustices which cause it. Those of us who live in affluent circumstances accept our duty to develop a simple lifestyle in order to contribute more generously to both relief and evangelism.

It may be said that paragraphs eight and nine bring us to the heart of the Covenant because they relate to world evangelization, which was the main theme of the International Congress at Lausanne. In these paragraphs, five segments of the human community are mentioned — churches, para-church agencies (i.e., independent agencies working alongside the church), unevangelized people, foreign missionaries, and the deprived, impoverished millions.

a. Churches

For about 150 years, since the dawn of the modern missionary movement at the beginning of the 19th century, Christendom was neatly divided between "sending churches" and "receiving churches." The sending churches were the older churches of the West (especially Europe and North America). And it was their missions which, under God, led to the birth and growth of younger churches who were at the receiving end. But now these distinctions are rapidly breaking down. *We rejoice that a new missionary era has dawned*, whose chief characteristic is what paragraph eight later calls *a growing partnership of churches*. On the one hand, *the dominant role of western missions is fast disappearing*, and with it the notion that missions anywhere in the world can be directed from some remote mission control in Europe, North America or elsewhere. On the other hand, *God is raising up from the younger churches a great new resource for world evangelization.* This phrase comes from Dr. Donald McGavran's paper. In it, he gave the startling figure of 200 Third World missionary societies with 3,400 missionaries reported in 1972 and more today. The All-Asia Mission Consultation's continuation committee have pledged to send out 10,000 Asian missionaries by the end of this century.

By this new missionary impetus from Asia, Africa and Latin America, God is *demonstrating that the responsibility to evangelize belongs to the whole body of Christ.* This plain biblical truth, which is beginning to be witnessed today, leads to a practical and demanding conclusion: *All churches* (whether young or old, whether large or small, whether in a developed or a developing country) *should therefore be asking God and themselves* a searching question, namely *what they should be doing both to reach their own area and to send missionaries to other parts of the world.* Some of the churches planted by the apostles seem almost immediately to have become centers of evangelistic witness (e.g., Rom 1:8; Phil. 1:5, 4: 15; I Thess. 1:6-8; cf., Acts 13:1-3). Moreover, it is not enough for a church to ask itself this question once, and then conveniently forget about it. No, *a re-evaluation of our missionary responsibility and role should be continuous.* Only then, when all churches conscientiously accept their God-given vocation, will *a growing partnership of churches* come to maturity, and *the universal character of Christ's church will be more clearly exhibited.*

b. Para-church Agencies

Although paragraph six has stated that God's "appointed means of spreading the Gospel" is the church, yet the Congress recognized the valid existence of para-church agencies. These do not (or should not) work in competition with the churches, but rather, being (in most cases) interdenominational in personnel and specialist in function, enable the churches to diversify their outreach. So *we thank God* for them. Some are seeking to extend the church by *evangelism* and *missions*, while others are seeking to deepen it by *theological education* and *church renewal.* Yet others concentrate on a particular means of communicating the Gospel like *Bible translation* (and distribution), *the mass media* (radio, television, journalism, etc.) and *Christian literature.* Even this is only a selection, for there are *other specialist fields* which are not mentioned. Although the right of such agencies to exist is agreed, and God is thanked for their work, yet the wisdom of their indefinite survival is not taken for granted. Like churches, para-church agencies should also *engage in constant self-examination* — in particular *to evaluate their effectiveness as part of the Church's mission.* Howard Snyder urged that "a clear distinction should be made between the church as the community of God's people and man-made structures." The Church is God's creation, essential and eternal; denominational and para-church agencies, however, being man's creation and expendable, cannot claim the same immortality. Some outlive their usefulness. In such cases voluntary termination is to be recommended.

c. Unevangelized people

Paragraph nine ("The Urgency of the Evangelistic Task") begins with the appalling statistic that *more than 2,700 million people*, representing *more than two-thirds of mankind, have yet to be evangelized.* That is, they have not yet heard the Good News of Jesus Christ. And this number keeps growing. The "population clock," started at the beginning of the Congress and stopped at its end, registered a world population increase of about one-and-a-half million people during those 10 days. The huge number of the unevangelized is more than a cold fact; it points the finger of accusation at us and forces us to acknowledge our guilty failure. *We are ashamed that so many have been neglected; it is a standing rebuke to us and to the whole church.* Such words can be written and spoken with comparative ease. But not until we get the unevangelized millions on our conscience, and take them to our heart in deep compassion will we stir ourselves to action.

Then another fact is stated, not to shame us but to encourage us, namely, that *now in many parts of the world* there is *an unprecedented receptivity to the Lord Jesus Christ.* Nobody has brought this fact to the church's attention more forcefully than Dr. Donald McGavran. In his paper at Lausanne he gave a few sample figures; e.g., the church in Taiwan had (by 1971) multiplied 20 times in 25 years, and in Africa south of the Sahara (according to Dr. David Barrett) there may well be 357 million Christians by the year 2000. Although in some parts of the world the door is still closed, in many parts of the world it is open, and the Holy Spirit is making millions receptive to Christ. We cannot be pessimistic. On the contrary, *we are convinced that this is the time for churches and para-church agencies to pray earnestly for the salvation of the unreached, and to launch new efforts to achieve world evangelization.* The great need is for Christians with the vision, the courage and the commitment to respond to this challenge and opportunity.

d. Foreign Missionaries

The Bangkok Conference, already mentioned in the commentary on paragraph five, gave currency to the idea of a moratorium (or suspension) of missionary funds and personnel. The call was not altogether understood and the word has become emotive. So the Covenant avoids the word, but clarifies the concept. It agrees that *a reduction of foreign missionaries and money . . . may sometimes be necessary.* But it qualifies this statement in three important ways.

First, such a situation is likely to arise only *in an evangelized country,* that is, when the primary, pioneer task of making the Gospel known has been done. Secondly, the purpose of such a reduction would be *to facilitate the national church's growth in self-reliance.* For it must be frankly acknowledged that foreign missionaries have sometimes stayed on too long in leadership roles in the national church, and in consequence have impeded the development of the church's own leaders, while the continued supply of foreign money has sometimes perpetuated in the national church a certain immature dependence. Thirdly, the ultimate objective of such a reduction of men and money would not be to reduce overall missionary advance, but to further it, for it would *release resources for unevangelized areas.* Our desire should be to increase the availability and mobility of missionaries, for *missionaries should flow ever more freely from and to all six continents.* We dare not impose any limit on the number of missionaries while so much of the world remains unevangelized — unless it be to exclude the wrong sort of missionaries. There is no room in today's church for the proud and the dominant, but only for those who will offer themselves *in a spirit of humble service.*

What, then, is our *goal?* It *should be, by all available means and at the earliest possible time* (no date is given), *that every person will have the opportunity to hear,* and not only to hear in some casual or superficial way, but so to hear as to *understand and,* by God's grace, *receive the Good News.*

e. The Impoverished Millions

The deprived, impoverished, undernourished people of
the world are introduced in the context of evangelism.
For the Covenant declares that *we cannot hope to attain
this goal* (of world evangelization) *without sacrifice.* But
it goes on to speak of both the plight of the poor and the
duty of the affluent. *All of us are shocked by the poverty
of millions and disturbed by the injustices which cause
it.* We may not all give an identical definition of justice
and injustice, or share the same economic theories and
remedies, or believe that God's will is an egalitarian society in which even the slightest differences of income and
possessions are not tolerated. But we are all appalled by
poverty, that is, by the immense numbers of people who
do not have enough to eat, whose shelter and clothing
are woefully inadequate, and whose opportunities for
education, employment and medical care are minimal.
Every sensitive Christian should be shocked by this situation and never grow so accustomed to it as to be un-
moved by it (Isa. 58:6,7).

Moreover, *those of us who live in affluent circumstances
accept* that we have a particular *duty.* This includes most
people in the West, where the average income is nearly
15 times more than the average in the developing world,
but also a small minority of rich Third World citizens.
Our duty is *to develop a simple life-style.* Perhaps no expression in the Covenant caused more anxious thought in
would-be signatories at Lausanne than this. What does it
mean for the affluent to develop a simple style of living?
Some have wished that the adjective were a comparative
and read "a simpler life-style." But even this would pose
problems for us: how much simpler? and, in any case,
simpler than what? The truth is that concepts like "poverty," "simplicity" and "generosity" are all relative
and are bound to mean different things to different people. For example, . . . running water, let alone constant
hot water, is regarded as a wonderful luxury by those
who have to queue for water at the village well, which
sometimes dries up. But in other parts of the world it can
hardly be regarded as incompatible with "a simple life-
style." Scripture lays down no absolute standards. On

the one hand, it gives no encouragement to an austere and negative asceticism, for it does not forbid the possession of private property (Acts 5:4), and it commands us to enjoy with gratitude the good gifts of our Creator (e.g., I Tim. 4:1-5; 6:17). On the other hand, it implies that some measure of equality is more pleasing to God then disparity, and its appeal to believers to be generous is based on the grace of our Lord Jesus Christ, because grace means generosity (II Cor. 8:8-15).

Every Christian should be content with the necessities of life (I Tim. 6:6-8), but every Christian must make his own conscientious decision before God where he draws the line between necessities and luxuries. It is certainly a sin to eat too much, and to waste food, especially when so many are starving. As for possessions, one way to decide whether we *need* something is to consider whether we *use* it, for we evidently do not need what we do not use. It would be at least a start if all of us went through our belongings (including our clothes) annually, in order to give away what we do not use. The paragraph concludes that the development of a simple life-style will not only be right in itself out of a caring solidarity with the poor, but will also enable us *to contribute more generously to both relief and evangelism,* for these good works are almost everywhere hampered by a shortage of money.

Questions for discussion:

1. "All churches should be asking God and themselves what they should be doing . . ." Complete the question from paragraph eight and then put it to your own church.
2. If you share in, or support, a para-church agency, can you evaluate its effectiveness?
3. Paragraph nine sets a goal. What is it? Can you make any personal contribution to its attainment?
4. "A simpler life-style." What might this mean for you?

The development of strategies for world evangelization calls for imaginative pioneering methods. Under God, the result will be the rise of churches deeply rooted in Christ and closely related to their culture. Culture must always be tested and judged by Scripture. Because man is God's creature, some of his culture is rich in beauty and goodness. Because he is fallen, all of it is tainted with sin and some of it is demonic. The Gospel does not presuppose the superiority of any culture to another, but evaluates all cultures according to its own criteria of truth and righteousness, and insists on moral absolutes in every culture. Missions have all too frequently exported with the Gospel an alien culture, and churches have sometimes been in bondage to culture rather than to the Scripture. Christ's evangelists must humbly seek to empty themselves of all but their personal authenticity in order to become the servants of others, and churches must seek to transform and enrich culture, all for the glory of God.

We confess that we have sometimes pursued church growth at the expense of church depth, and divorced evangelism from Christian nurture. We also acknowledge that some of our missions have been too slow to equip and encourage national leaders to assume their rightful responsibilities. Yet we are committed to indigenous principles, and long that every church will have national leaders who manifest a Christian style of leadership in terms not of domination but of service. We recognize that there is a great need to improve theological education, especially for church leaders. In every nation and culture there should be an effective training program for pastors and laymen in doctrine, discipleship, evangelism, nurture and service. Such training programs should not rely on any stereotyped methodology but should be developed by creative local initiatives according to biblical standards.

Paragraphs ten and eleven handle two related subjects, culture and leadership. Both have to do with churches which come into being as the fruit of missionary labor. For *the development of strategies for world evangelization,* calling for *imaginative pioneering methods,* will *under God . . .result . . . in the rise of churches.* What should be the relation of these churches to culture? What kind of leadership should they have?

a. Culture

Culture was a major topic of thought and discussion at Lausanne. But the word is difficult to define. Culture may be likened to a tapestry, intricate and often beautiful, which is woven by a given society to express its corporate identity. The colors and patterns of the tapestry are the community's common beliefs and common customs, inherited from the past, enriched by contemporary art and binding the community together. Each of us, without exception, has been born and bred in a particular culture. Being part of our upbringing and environment, it is also part of ourselves, and we find it very difficult to stand outside it and evaluate it christianly. Yet this we must learn to do. For if Jesus Christ is to be Lord of all, our cultural heritage cannot be excluded from his Lordship. And this applies to churches as well as individuals.

The churches which arise in every place are bound to have a double orientation, towards Christ and towards culture. They cannot escape the responsibility to develop an attitude to both. What should it be? An earlier draft of the Covenant described churches as "rooted in Christ and in culture." But it was correctly pointed out that the roots of a church are in Christ alone. So the draft was amended to portray churches as *rooted in Christ and closely related to their culture.* Now Christ and culture are sometimes in conflict. What does the Covenant have to say about this? First, it insists on the proper evaluation of culture. Secondly, it gives examples of the dangerous influence of culture when it is not properly evaluated.

(i.) *The evaluation of culture. Culture must always be tested and judged by Scripture.* This is because culture is the product of human society, whereas Scripture is the product of divine revelation; and Jesus was emphatic that God's Word must always take precedence over man's traditions (Mark 7:8,9,13). Not that all culture is bad. Culture is ambiguous because man is ambiguous. Man is both noble (because made in God's image) and ignoble (because fallen and sinful). And his culture faithfully reflects these two aspects of man. *Because man is God's creature, some of his culture is rich in beauty and goodness.* Man's total depravity means that every part of him has been affected by the fall; it does not mean that he is incapable of anything good, beautiful or true. On the contrary, Jesus himself said that evil men can do good things (Matt. 7:11; cf., Luke 6:32). And the beauty of man's artistic achievement bears witness to the creativity with which his Creator has endowed him (Gen. 4:21,22). On the other hand, because man *has fallen, all* his culture *is tainted with sin and some of it is demonic,* that is, actually inspired by the devil and the powers of darkness.

So then, because of its ambiguous nature, all culture must be tested. *The Gospel does not presuppose the superiority of any culture to another.* In matters which are morally neutral, cultures are simply different from one another, rather than superior or inferior to each other. When we travel, for example, we have no liberty to assume that our way of doing things (the way we talk, dress, eat, greet people, organize our program, etc.) is necessarily better than other people's. "According to the Bible," said Dr. McGavran at Lausanne, "God has no favorite among cultures. He accepts them all" (Rev. 21:26, but cf., v.27).

What, then, is the relation of the Gospel to culture? It *evaluates all cultures according to its own criteria of truth and righteousness.* It rejects, for example, any idolatry which denies the uniqueness of God, any merit-system which denies the need of grace, and any oppression which denies the dignity of man. And it insists *on moral absolutes in every culture.* For although human customs are relative in value, God's moral law is absolute and invariable.

(ii.) *The influence of culture.* Having insisted that all culture must be tested by Scripture, paragraph ten goes on to give some examples of our failure to do this. The principle is applied to missions, churches and evangelists. *Missions have all too frequently exported with the Gospel an alien culture.* That is, their message and manner of life have been partly biblical, partly cultural. Dr. René Padilla was particularly outspoken in his paper on the harmfulness of what he called "culture Christianity," namely, "the identification of Christianity with culture or a cultural expression." He referred both to European colonialism and to the American way of life, but was careful to point out that other examples could be given. Certainly, the younger churches of the Third World know the painful trauma which some missions have caused by their failure to distinguish between their Gospel and their culture. The apostle Paul, far from imposing an alien culture on others, adapted himself to their culture, becoming "all things to all men" (I Cor. 9:19-23).

If younger churches have been confused by the importation of an alien culture, they have a second problem in knowing how to relate to their own national or tribal culture. Here the truth is that not only missions but also *churches have sometimes been in bondage to culture rather than to Scripture.* Yet if some have been too subservient to their local culture, others have been too critical of it, and have failed to develop any music, liturgy, art, architecture, or literature in their own national idiom. Churches should even go beyond reacting to the culture that is already there, and should take initiatives to influence it. *Churches must seek to transform and enrich culture, all for the glory of God.*

The third example concerns *Christ's evangelists*, especially those called to cross-cultural missionary work, who find it hard to renounce their own culture and adapt themselves to the culture of those among whom they live and labor. Yet, following the example of the Son of God who "emptied himself" of his glory in order to serve (Phil. 2: 5-7), Christ's evangelists are called *humbly to seek to empty themselves* of their cultural status, power, privileges and prejudices, indeed *of all but their personal authenticity.* Such self-humbling, self-emptying and self-giving will be *in order to become the servants of others (II Cor. 4:5).*

b. Leadership

Paragraph eleven, "Education and Leadership," opens with a frank double confession. First, *we confess that we have sometimes pursued church growth at the expense of church depth, and divorced evangelism from Christian*

46

nurture. As a result, it is not an exaggeration to say that Christian superficiality has become a worldwide phenomenon. Many converts never grow up in Christ. Secondly, we *acknowledge that some of our missions have been too slow to equip and encourage national leaders to assume their rightful responsibilities.* This, too, is a fact of missionary history. The transition from a mission situation to a church situation has too often been marred by a reluctance to hand over the leadership to nationals.

It is significant that the apostle Paul, who might be described as the greatest Christian missionary of all time, made neither of these two mistakes. His great ambition, he wrote, was not just to win converts but to "present every man mature in Christ" (Col. 1:28,29), and it was his practice from the first missionary journey onwards to appoint local leaders as elders in every church (Acts 14:23).

(i.) *Principles of leadership.* The Covenant mentions two essential principles of Christian leadership. First, *we are committed to indigenous principles,* that is, to the vision of an autonomous church with national (as opposed to foreign) leadership, and we *long that every church will have national leaders.* Paul instructed Titus to "appoint elders in every town" (Tit. 1:5), and presumably they were local men. The second principle concerns the kind of leadership which nationals will give. Being equally the children of Adam, national leaders are no more immune than missionaries to the sins of pride, power-hunger, and pomposity. So our longing is for national leaders *who manifest a Christian style of leadership,* drawing their inspiration not from secular government but from Christ's teaching and example, a leadership *in terms not of domination but of service* (Mark 10:42-45 cf., II Cor. 4:5; I Pet. 5:3).

(ii.) *Training for leadership. There is a great need to improve theological education, especially for church leaders.* The problems facing the church are always basically theological. Therefore, the church needs leaders who have learned to think theologically, so that they can apply Christian principles to every situation. This is also true of pastors who as the church's teachers not only need to be "apt teachers" (I Tim. 3:2) but "must hold firm to the sure word as taught" so that they may be able "to give instruction in sound doctrine, and also to confute those who contradict it" (Tit. 1:9). So there was much discussion at Lausanne about the strategic need to develop, especially but not exclusively in the Third World, evangelical seminaries, theological education by extension, research centers, regional and national theological fellowships, and the exchange of theological teachers.

Church leaders include lay leaders. Clericalism (the suppression of the laity by the clergy) is not only incompatible with the biblical doctrine of the church as the people of God but hinders the work of the church by denying it gifted leadership which God has provided. Yet lay leaders also need training (Eph. 4:11,12). So one of the most urgent needs of the day is the availability *in every nation and culture* of a really *effective training program for pastor and laymen.*

Such a program will have at least two characteristics. First, it will be thorough, and should include in its syllabus not only *doctrine* (biblical theology) but also the outworking of doctrine in *discipleship, evangelism, nurture and service.* Secondly, it will be indigenous like the leadership being trained by it. It should not be imposed from outside but *developed by . . . local initiatives.* Nor should it *rely on any stereotyped methodology,* since the local initiatives should be *creative.* When such initiatives, besides being local and creative, are also truly submissive to *biblical standards,* the result should be a training program of enormous benefit to the church.

Questions for study:

1. What are some of the major ingredients of your local culture? Isolate those parts of it which you think should be (a) accepted, (b) judged, (c) transformed and enriched?

2. Paragraph ten talks about evangelists as "servants of others" and paragraph eleven about leadership in terms of "service." Discuss the relation between authority and service in a leadership role.

3. "Christian nurture." What steps does your church take to nurture new converts?

4. "An effective training program for . . . laymen." Supposing you had the responsibility to arrange one, what would it be like?

CONFLICT AND PERSECUTION *We believe that we are engaged in constant spiritual warfare with the principalities and powers of evil, who are seeking to overthrow the church and frustrate its task of world evangelization. We know our need to equip ourselves with God's armor and to fight this battle with the spiritual weapons of truth and prayer. For we detect the activity of our enemy, not only in false ideologies outside the church, but also inside it in false gospels which twist Scripture and put man in the place of God. We need both watchfulness and discernment to safeguard the biblical Gospel. We acknowledge that we ourselves are not immune to worldliness of thought and action, that is, to a surrender to secularism. For example, although careful studies of church growth, both numerical and spiritual, are right and valuable, we have sometimes neglected them. At other times, desirous to insure a response to the Gospel, we have compromised our message, manipulated our hearers through pressure techniques, and become unduly preoccupied with statistics or even dishonest in our use of them. All this is worldly. The church must be in the world; the world must not be in the church.*

It is the God-appointed duty of every government to secure conditions of peace, justice and liberty in which the church may obey God, serve the Lord Christ, and preach the Gospel without interference. We therefore pray for the leaders of the nations and call upon them to guarantee freedom of thought and conscience, and freedom to practice and propagate religion in accordance with the will of God and as set forth in The Universal Declaration of Human Rights. We also express our deep concern for all who have been unjustly imprisoned, and especially for our brethren who are suffering for their testimony to the Lord Jesus. We promise to pray and work for their freedom. At the same time we refuse to be intimidated by their fate. God helping us, we too will seek to stand against injustice and to remain faithful to the Gospel, whatever the cost. We do not forget the warnings of Jesus that persecution is inevitable.

Paragraphs 12 and 13 introduce into the Covenant a somber note, namely, that the church must expect fierce opposition. True, Jesus promised that he would build his church on the rock and that not even the powers of

Hades (death) would be able to overcome it (Matt. 16:18). The church has an eternal destiny, and even in time is secure in the hand of its sovereign Lord (Acts 4:24-28). Yet Jesus also warned us that we would encounter much hostility (e.g., John 15:18; 16:4), which would be stirred up by that wicked spirit he called "the ruler of this world" (John 12:31; 14:30; 16:11).

So paragraph 12, "Spiritual Conflict," begins with the statement of two facts, first about the battle we have to fight, and secondly about the armor we need to wear. First, *we believe that we are engaged in constant spiritual warfare with the principalities and powers of evil.* The church has human enemies, but behind them lurk "spiritual hosts of wickedness" (Eph. 6:12), as subtle as they are unscrupulous, and with them our warfare must be unremitting. For they are *seeking to overthrow the church and frustrate its task of world evangelization* (II Cor. 4:3,4). Yet we could never hope to resist them, let alone defeat them, in our puny human strength. The church is no match for the devil. So *we know our need to equip ourselves with God's armor* (Eph. 6:10-17) *and to fight this battle with . . . spiritual weapons* (II Cor. 10:3-5), especially the mighty weapons *of truth and prayer.* As for the power of truth, we need to remember Paul's conviction that "we cannot do anything against the truth, but only for the truth" (II Cor. 13:8). As for the power of prayer, Jesus said that he himself used this weapon against Satan (Luke 22:31,32).

After this general introduction to *spiritual warfare* and *spiritual weapons,* the paragraph goes on to particularize. It dares to state that we are able to *detect the activity of our enemy.* Although he is himself invisible, his tactics are not, and so we are "not ignorant of his designs" (II Cor. 2:11). We know from Scripture what weapons he used in his attack upon the early church, and we know from history and experience that his methods have not changed. The three chief weapons of his armory are still error, worldliness and persecution.

a. Error

Jesus called the devil "a liar and the father of lies" (John 8:44). He hates the truth and is constantly seeking to deceive men into error. Thus, we do not hesitate to attribute to his malevolent work *false ideologies outside the church*. Indeed, it would be impossible to understand how intelligent, educated people can believe some of the nonsense taught by non-Christian systems and cults if it were not for the work of deceiving spirits (I John 2: 18-26; 4:1-3). But the devil does not limit his activity to the sphere outside the church. It is grievous to have to add that he is also responsible for *false gospels . . . inside it*. Paul rejected the message of the Judaizers as a false gospel (Gal. 1:6-9), and there are false teachers who trouble the church with false gospels today. How may they be recognized?

In two main ways. First, they *twist Scripture* (cf., II Cor. 2: 17; 4:2 and II Pet. 3:15,16). Far from desiring to be submissive to its authority and its message, they presume to stand in judgment on it and to distort its plain meaning to favor their own unbiblical presuppositions. The second of their characteristics is such an unbounded confidence in man and his abilities as virtually to *put man in the place of God*. "Godliness," or a due reverence for God, is always a mark of true religion (I Tim. 4:7; II Tim. 2:16; Tit. 1:1), whereas the attempted deification of man was the essence of the first sin ("you will be like God" Gen. 3:5) and remains the essence of all sin today. It is true that man has unique dignity as the only creature made in God's image, but he is still a creature, and a sinner too, dependent on God's grace. A good test of every ideology is whether it exalts God and humbles man, or whether it exalts man and dethrones God. *We need both watchfulness* ("be watchful, stand firm in your faith!" I Cor. 16:13) *and discernment* ("test the spirits to see whether they are of God," I John 4:1) if we are *to safeguard the biblical Gospel*. Christ and his apostles regularly warned us of false teachers (e.g., Matt. 7:15 ff; Acts 20:29 ff; II Pet. 2; I John 2:18 ff); we need to be constantly on our guard.

b. Worldliness

The devil uses moral as well as intellectual weapons. If he cannot deceive the church into error, he will attempt to corrupt it with sin and worldliness. This part of the paragraph has a particular application to us as evangelical Christians. We may by God's grace be kept faithful to the biblical Gospel; yet *we acknowledge that we ourselves are not immune* to the onslaught of Satan, especially *to worldliness of thought and action.* Worldliness has often been defined in our evangelical circles in relation to questionable habits like smoking, drinking, dancing, and going to the movies. And indeed all of us have to make up our mind conscientiously about these and similar practices. But worldliness is something far more subtle. "The world" means secular or Christless society, and "worldliness" is its outlook, *a surrender to secularism* in either our thinking or our behavior.

The paragraph goes on to cite as an example of worldliness our attitude to *careful studies of church growth, both numerical and spiritual. We have sometimes neglected them,* it says, as if we really did not care whether our church was growing in either size or depth. Such indifference and neglect are signs of worldliness, for these studies *are right and valuable. At other times,* we have made the opposite mistake. The numerical growth of the church has become almost an obsession with us. And therefore, *desirous* (even determined) *to insure a response to the Gospel,* we have resorted to doubtful methods, which Paul would almost certainly have included in the "disgraceful underhanded ways" which he said he had renounced (II Cor. 4:2). Either *we have compromised our message* ("tampered with God's Word" II Cor. 4:2), eliminating such unfashionable elements as self-denial and judgment in order to make it more palatable to modern man; or we have *manipulated our hearers through pressure techniques,* which is to treat human beings as less than human; or we have *become unduly preoccupied with statistics* (as if the work of the Holy Spirit of God could ever be reduced to mere statistics!), or *even dishonest in our use of them* (publishing reports which are not strictly true). It is an ugly list of misdemeanors. *All this is worldly.* Wherever it is found, it indicates that somehow the devil has insinuated a worldly perspective into the church, and so has succeeded in getting things the wrong way round. *The church must be in the world; the world must not be in the church* (John 17:15).

c. Persecution

Not content with his attempts to introduce sin and error into the church, the devil also attacks the church from outside, seeking either by physical persecution or by restrictive legislation to hinder the church's work. So paragraph 13, "Freedom and Persecution," boldly grasps the thorny issue of relations between church and state. It recognizes that each has a duty to the other, and it expounds these duties with special reference to I Tim. 2, verses 1-4.

It is the God-appointed duty of every government to secure conditions of peace, justice and liberty. For then "we may lead a quiet and peaceable life, godly and respectful in every way" (v.2). In such conditions *the church may obey God* ("godly"), serve the Lord Christ (Col. 3:24; no Christian who has confessed, "Jesus is Lord" can also declare, "Caesar is Lord," cf., Mark 12:17) *and preach the Gospel without interference* (implied in verses 3 and 4, cf., Acts 4:19; 5:29).

The church also has a responsibility to the state, and in particular *to pray for the leaders of the nations* (verse 1 and 2a). The church cannot stop with prayer, however. In addition it has a duty, insofar as it is able, to be the nation's conscience, and to remind leaders of their God-ordained role. Therefore, we not only call upon God for our leaders, but *we call upon* our leaders themselves *to guarantee freedom of thought and conscience, and freedom to practice and propagate religion.* These freedoms have been *set forth in the Universal Declaration of Human Rights,* which was unanimously adopted by the General Assembly of the United Nations in December, 1948, with eight abstentions.

Article 18 reads, "Everyone has the right to freedom of thought, conscience and religion; this right includes freedom to change his religion or belief; and freedom, either alone or in community with others, and in public or private, to manifest his religion or belief in teaching, practice, worship or observance."

More important still, the guarantee of these freedoms is *in accordance with the will of God,* for he has instituted "governing authorities" to punish criminals and reward good citizens, not to curtail legitimate freedoms, still less to tyrannize the innocent (Rom. 13:1 ff).

Having outlined the reciprocal duties of church and state, the paragraph turns its attention to the victims of oppression. *We also express our deep concern for all who have been unjustly imprisoned.* We do not call them "prisoners of conscience," for some men's conscience is too perverted to be a reliable guide. We are thinking rather of those victims of tyranny who have neither done nor plotted any harm, but have been imprisoned either merely for their opinions, or for actions within the freedoms mentioned above. Among such we mention *especially our brethren who are suffering for their testimony to the Lord Jesus* (Rev. 1:9). We have been commanded to remember them and even to feel for them "as though in prison with them" (Heb. 13:3). Sympathy, however, is not enough; *we promise to pray and work for their freedom* (cf., Luke 4:18).

There is one thing more to say, and this is that *we refuse to be intimidated by their fate.* Oppressors have always imagined that they could use violence to assert their will and crush the church. They have never been able to, and they never will. Although we know our human frailty, yet, *God helping us, we too will seek to stand against injustice and to remain faithful to the Gospel, whatever the cost.* No doubt it costs most of us nothing to say this, but at least we recognize the real possibility of tyranny and persecution spreading into countries which at present are free. For *we do not forget the warnings of Jesus that persecution is inevitable* (e.g., Matt. 5:10-12).

Questions for study:

1. Read Ephesians 6:10-20. What does this teach about Christian warfare and Christian weapons?

2. "We detect the activity of our enemy." Do you? Where does he seem to you to be most active today?

3. Some examples are given at the end of paragraph 12 of the worldliness of the church. Do any of them fit your situation? Can you add to the list?

4. Can you think of any practical action you or your church could take (a) in appealing to national leaders, and (b) in working for the release of prisoners?

THE POWER OF THE SPIRIT AND THE RETURN OF CHRIST

We believe in the power of the Holy Spirit. The Father sent his Spirit to bear witness to his Son; without his witness ours is futile. Conviction of sin, faith in Christ, new birth and Christian growth are all his work. Further, the Holy Spirit is a missionary spirit; thus evangelism will become a realistic possibility only when the Spirit renews the church in truth and wisdom, faith, holiness, love and power. We therefore call upon all Christians to pray for such a visitation of the sovereign Spirit of God that all his fruit may appear in all his people and that all his gifts may enrich the body of Christ. Only then will the whole church become a fit instrument in his hands, that the whole earth may hear his voice.

We believe that Jesus Christ will return personally and visibly, in power and glory, to consummate his salvation and his judgment. This promise of his coming is a further spur to our evangelism, for we remember his words that the Gospel must first be preached to all nations. We believe that the interim period between Christ's ascension and return is to be filled with the mission of the people of God, who have no liberty to stop before the End. We also remember his warning that false Christs and false prophets will arise as precursors of the final Antichrist. We therefore reject as a proud, self-confident dream the notion that man can ever build a utopia on earth. Our Christian confidence is that God will perfect his kingdom, and we look forward with eager anticipation to that day, and to the new heaven and earth in which righteousness will dwell and God will reign forever. Meanwhile, we rededicate ourselves to the service of Christ and of men in joyful submission to his authority over the whole of our lives.

The last two paragraphs of the Covenant emphasize two neglected dimensions of evangelism. One is the only ground on which we can hope for results (the power of the Holy Spirit); the other is the ultimate goal to which we look (the return of Jesus Christ). These are great Christian doctrines concerning the second and third persons of the Trinity, so each paragraph begins with an affirmation of faith: *We believe in the power of the Holy Spirit . . . We believe that Jesus Christ will return . . .*

Happy is the church which is fortified by these assurances; wretched indeed are those who lack them!

a. The Power of the Holy Spirit

After a reminder of the malicious, destructive power of the devil (paragraph 12), it is an appropriate relief to turn our thoughts to the gracious and constructive power of the Holy Spirit. Again and again Scripture links the Spirit with power. In the Old Testament, it is "not by might, nor by power, but by my Spirit, says the Lord of hosts" (Zech. 4:6). In the New Testament Jesus himself spoke of the power of the Spirit for witness (Acts 1:8) and the apostle Paul wrote that, conscious of his own weakness, he relied in his ministry on the "demonstration of the Spirit and power" (I Cor. 2:3-5, cf., I Thess. 1:5). We must do the same.

The particular spheres mentioned in which the Holy Spirit's power is needed are: first, the witness of the church; and, secondly, the renewal of the church.

(i.) *The witness of the church.* We are reminded that *the Father sent his Spirit to bear witness to his Son.* This is an echo of the Trinitarian teaching of Jesus in the Upper Room. He emphasized that the distinctive work of the Spirit whom the Father was going to send would be in relation to himself, the Son; that the Spirit would delight above all else to glorify or manifest the Son (John 16:14); and that therefore in the spread of the Gospel the Holy Spirit would be the chief witness. "He will bear witness to me." Only after saying this did Jesus add to his apostles, "and you also are witnesses" (John 15:26,27). Once we have grasped the significance of this order, we shall have no difficulty in agreeing that *without his witness ours is futile.*

All four main stages in the great event we call conversion are the work of the Holy Spirit. First, *conviction of sin.* It is the Spirit, Jesus said, who would "convince the world of sin and of righteousness and of judgment" (John 16:8-11). Next, *faith in Christ.* It is the Spirit who opens the eyes of convicted sinners to see in Jesus their Savior and Lord, and to believe in him, for "no one can say, 'Jesus is Lord' except by the Holy Spirit" (I Cor. 12:3). Thirdly, the *new birth* is a birth "of the

Spirit" (John 3:6-8). Fourthly, *Christian growth* or sanctification is his work too (II Cor. 3:18). So the power of the Holy Spirit in evangelism is not optional, but indispensable.

The work of the Spirit arises from his nature. *The Holy Spirit is a missionary Spirit,* and this is the reason why *evangelism,* instead of being imposed by constraint, *should arise spontaneously from a Spirit-filled church.* Since the Spirit is a missionary Spirit, it follows that a Spirit-filled church becomes a missionary church, as we see clearly in the book of Acts. *A church that is not a missionary church,* but instead is preoccupied with its own affairs, *is contradicting itself,* contradicting its very nature as an outward-looking missionary community, and is also *quenching the Spirit* who longs to flow forth from his people into the world like "rivers of living water" into a desert (John 7:37-39; I Thess. 5:19). Only the Spirit can turn introverted churches inside out.

(ii.) *The renewal of the church.* What has been said so far about the church's witness, evangelism and missionary zeal is in many parts of the world more a theory than a reality. So it is recognized that *worldwide evangelization will become a realistic possibility only when the Spirit renews the church.* There is a lot of talk about the renewal of the church today. But some who broach the subject have a rather restricted aspiration. They concentrate their concern on the renewal of the church's unity, or the church's structures, or the church's experience of spiritual gifts. The Covenant paints on a broader canvas, however, and longs for the Spirit to renew the church in every way, *in truth* (as at the Reformation) *and wisdom,* in *faith, holiness, love, and power.* For such a total and wholesome renewal we need to pray. True, the Holy Spirit is a sovereign Spirit and cannot be commanded or organized. Nevertheless, he graciously hears his people's prayers. So *we call upon all Christians to pray for . . . a visitation of the sovereign Spirit of God.* The word "visitation" is used here as Scripture sometimes uses it to indicate special manifestations of God's presence and special activities of God's power. For example, although God is constantly present and active in his world, he is said to "visit" the earth when he enriches it with rain and prepares it for the harvest (Psa. 65:9). So too we may say that the Holy Spirit, who indwells and never forsakes his people, yet "visits" them whenever he puts forth his power on their behalf. And our confidence is that when he visits the church in power he will both bear his fruit (the nine Christian graces listed in Galatians 5:22,23) and bestow his gifts (some 20 of which are mentioned in Romans 12:3-8, I Corinthians 12:4-31, and Ephesians 4:11). So we pray for *such a visitation* of the Spirit that *all his fruit may appear in all his people* (since all nine qualities are to characterize us) and that *all his gifts may enrich the body of Christ* (since they are service gifts bestowed "for the common good" and distributed to different believers "as he wills" I Cor. 12:7,11).

The paragraph ends with the conviction that *only then,* when the Holy Spirit is free to move with power, *will the whole church become a fit instrument in his hands,* so that, in words which take up the Congress theme, *the whole earth may hear his voice* (Psa. 67:1-3).

b. The Return of Jesus Christ

For many centuries the universal church believed in the second advent, and all Christians could recite the relevent clause of the Nicene Creed ("And he shall come again with glory to judge both the quick and the dead") without any mental reservations or any need surreptitiously to cross their fingers. But now scientific secularism has eroded the historic faith of the church, and the cry has arisen to demythologize this article of the creed. Against this background of unbelief, the biblical faith of the Congress participants stands out in bold relief: *We believe that Jesus Christ will return.* And although evangelical Christians, anxious not to go beyond the plain assertions of the Bible, retain a humble agnosticism about some of the details of the Lord's return, we are able to affirm at least four truths about it.

First, he will return *personally,* for the one who is coming is "this Jesus" whom the apostles saw ascend into heaven (Acts 1:11). Secondly, he will return *visibly,* so that "every eye will see him" (Rev. 1:7). Thirdly, in striking contrast to the manner of his first coming, he will return *in power and glory.* The very words are borrowed from Jesus who said, "They will see the Son of man coming in clouds with great power and glory" (Mark 13: 26). Fourthly, he is coming *to consummate his salvation and judgment,* for both processes began with his first coming and both will be completed at his second (John 5: 21-29; Heb. 9:27,28). All Christians should be looking and longing for Christ to come, and should share this great confidence that his coming will be personal, visible, glorious and final.

This promise of his coming is not a piece of unpractical theologizing. On the contrary, Christ and his apostles never spoke of it to satisfy idle curiosity, but always to stimulate practical action. In particular, it is *a further spur to our evangelism.* For he himself forged a link between our proclamation and his return, and *we remember his words that the Gospel must first be preached to all nations* "and then the end will come" (Matt. 24:14). So *the interim period* between his two comings, *between Christ's ascension and return,* is by his own appointment *to be filled with the mission of the people of God.* "Go . . . and make disciples of all nations . . .," he said, "and lo I am with you always, to the close of the age" (Matt. 28:19,20; Acts 1:8-11). Thus, *we have no liberty to stop before the End.*

There follows a clarification. What exactly is the church's expectation or hope? Some speak nowadays as if we should expect the world to get better and better, and as if to secure conditions of material prosperity, international peace, social justice, political freedom and personal fulfillment is equivalent to establishing the kingdom of God. Certainly, it is our duty to work for justice and freedom, as was stated in paragraph five. And certainly too, in God's providence and common grace we can expect some success. But Jesus gave us no expectation that everything would get steadily better. On the contrary, *we remember his warning* that the coming of Christ will be preceded by the coming of Anti-Christ, and *that false Christs and false prophets will arise as precursors of the final Anti-Christ. (Mark 13:21-23; I John 2:18; 4:1-3). We therefore reject as a proud, self-confident dream,* and as entirely at variance with the teaching of Jesus, *the notion that man can ever build a utopia on earth.* This is simply not the Christian hope according to Scripture. *Our Christian confidence is that God will perfect his kingdom,* for Jesus always spoke of the kingdom as God's gift, not man's achievement (Luke 12:32).

Professor Peter Beyerhaus distinguished clearly in his paper on "World Evangelization and the Kingdom of God" between two stages of the kingdom, and argued that evangelization is both "inviting into the kingdom of grace" now and "preparing for the kingdom of glory" to come. Men enter the kingdom of grace today by spiritual regeneration and should become "convincing models of social and political involvement." But the total redemption of man, society and creation awaits the kingdom of glory. This eschatological vision "has inspired many missionaries with a holy restlessness" as they long for Christ's promise to be fulfilled. And although we may differ from one another in the precise form we expect his kingdom to take, yet all of us *look forward with eager anticipation to that day, and to the new heaven and earth,* which are clearly promised, *in which righteousness will dwell and God will reign forever* (Rev. 21:1-5; II Pet. 3: 13).

From this glorious vision of the future we turn back to the concrete realities of the present. Indeed, it is our Christian hope which inspires us always to abound in the work of the Lord, because we know that our labor will not be in vain (I Cor. 15:58). So *meanwhile,* as we patiently await the consummation, *we rededicate ourselves to the service of Christ and of men in joyful submission to his authority over the whole of our lives* (Matt. 28:18).

Questions for study:

1. It is easy to talk about the power of the Holy Spirit in evangelism. But what does it mean in practice to rely on his power rather than our own?

2. The renewal of the church is much discussed today. What is it? How will it happen?

3. Does the promise of Christ's return make any difference to your life?

4. What is the kingdom of God? How does it spread? How will it be consummated?

CONCLUSION *Therefore, in the light of this our faith and our resolve, we enter into a solemn covenant with God and with each other, to pray, to plan and to work together for the evangelization of the whole world. We call upon others to join us. May God help us by his grace and for his glory to be faithful to this our covenant! Amen, Alleluia!*

The declaration so far made has consisted partly of affirmation (what we believe) and partly of determination (what we intend to do); in other words, partly of faith, partly of resolve. *Therefore*, we conclude, it is *in the light of this our faith and our resolve* that we frame our Covenant or binding promise. *We enter into a solemn Covenant with God and with each other*, first *to pray* together, secondly *to plan* together, and thirdly *to work together* (in that order of priority) *for the evangelization of the whole world*, that is to say, to bring the Good News within meaningful reach of the whole population of the earth. It is a colossal undertaking. Indeed, without the mobilization of the church, and especially without the grace of God, it is a hopeless undertaking. So *we call upon others to join us*, hoping that many besides the original signatories at Lausanne will thoughtfully consider and sign the Covenant. Above all, we pray that God will enable us to be faithful. We know our weakness, and put no confidence in ourselves. Our only hope of remaining faithful lies in his grace, and our supreme motivation is his greater glory. Therefore our prayer is that *God* will *help us by his grace and for his glory to be faithful to this our Covenant. Amen. Alleluia!*